Thune's Journey From Murdo to the Senate

A Life of Leadership, Legacy, and Public Service in South Dakota

Beatrice G. George

Table Of Contents

Introduction

Chapter One: Early Life and Education
Building a Foundation Through Education
Shaping a Vision for the Future

Chapter Two: Background
The Thune Family Legacy
Life in Murdo
The Role of Mentorship and Community Leaders

Chapter Three: Academic Achievements
Biola University: A Broader Perspective
The Influence of Education on Leadership
A Legacy Rooted in Learning
Chapter Four: Personal Experience

Early Professional Challenges and Growth
Family Life and its Impact on Leadership
Personal Growth Through Challenges

Chapter Five: Early Career
Working with Jim Abdnor: A Transformative Start
Return to South Dakota: State-Level Engagement
Building Relationships and Networks

Chapter Six: Political Journey
A Humble Beginning in Public Service
Establishing a Reputation in the Senate
The Road to Majority Leader

Chapter Seven: Political Career
U.S. House of Representatives: 1997–2003
Legislative Achievements

Majority Leader: A New Era of Leadership

Chapter Eight : Net Worth
Early Financial Foundation
Wealth Transparency and Ethics
A Financial Legacy of Integrity

Chapter Nine: Legacy and Influence
Tax Reform and Economic Policy
Influence Within the Republican Party

Chapter Ten: Personal Life
Family Life and Marriage

Chapter Eleven: Impact
Economic Impact
Social and Cultural Impact
Impact on South Dakota

Conclusion

Introduction

John Thune's journey in American politics exemplifies steadfast dedication to public service, strategic leadership, and a deep-rooted commitment to representing his constituents. Born on January 7, 1961, in the small town of Murdo, South Dakota, Thune has carved a path that bridges the values of rural America with the demands of national governance. As a leading figure in the U.S.

Senate and a key member of the Republican Party, he has become synonymous with principled conservatism and pragmatic policy-making. For decades, Thune has stood as a voice for his state and a prominent player in shaping national policy. His political ascent began with humble beginnings, fueled by a chance encounter with Congressman Jim Abdnor during a high school basketball game. This seemingly minor moment ignited a spark in the young Thune, setting him on a trajectory that would eventually take him to Capitol Hill. This early inspiration, combined with a commitment to his community, led him to pursue an education at Biola University and later earn an MBA from the University of South Dakota.

These academic achievements not only honed his intellectual skills but also prepared him for the complexities of governance. Thune's early professional years were marked by roles that combined public service with administrative expertise. Working for Jim Abdnor in Washington, D.C., and later at the Small Business Administration during President Reagan's administration, he gained invaluable insights into the workings of federal government institutions.

These roles allowed him to understand the intricate balance between serving local interests and navigating national priorities, a balance he would master throughout his career. In 1996, South Dakotans entrusted Thune with a seat in the U.S. House of Representatives. Over the course of three terms, he distinguished himself as a steadfast advocate for his home state, championing issues that resonated with his constituents. However, it was his 2004 victory in the U.S. Senate race that cemented his reputation as a formidable figure in American politics. Unseating the-Senate Minority Leader Tom Daschle in a closely watched contest, Thune's victory reverberated nationwide, highlighting his political acumen and the depth of his support in South Dakota.

Since taking office in 2005, Thune has consistently been a driving force behind key legislative initiatives. His expertise in tax policy, rural development, and infrastructure has shaped critical bills, earning him recognition as a strategic policymaker. Within the Senate, Thune's influence has steadily grown, culminating in his election as Senate Majority Leader in January 2025. In this role, he has taken the reins from Mitch McConnell, becoming the second South Dakotan in history to hold such a powerful position.

Beyond the legislative chamber, Thune's leadership style has been characterized by a focus on collaboration, a willingness to engage across the aisle, and a steadfast adherence to his principles. He has navigated complex political landscapes with grace, balancing the expectations of a polarized electorate while remaining true to his core values. This ability to find common ground without compromising his beliefs has earned him respect across the political spectrum. Yet, John Thune's story extends beyond his professional achievements. A devoted husband to Kimberley Weems and father to two daughters, Thune's personal life reflects the values he champions in public service.

Whether jogging through Sioux Falls or attending community events, he remains deeply connected to the people he represents. His humility, often described as a hallmark of his character, resonates with constituents who see in him a reflection of their own aspirations and challenges. This biography seeks to explore the multifaceted life of John Thune, tracing his evolution from a small-town boy with big dreams to a statesman of national renown.

It will delve into the experiences that shaped his worldview, the policies he championed, and the legacy he continues to build. Through the lens of his personal and professional journey, readers will gain a deeper understanding of the man behind the title and the enduring impact of his leadership. As the pages unfold, Thune's unwavering dedication to service, his strategic brilliance, and his grounded approach to politics will come to life. This is not just a story about a politician; it is a testament to the power of perseverance, integrity, and the enduring influence of those who dare to lead.

Chapter One: Early Life and Education

John Thune's life story begins in the rural landscapes of Murdo, South Dakota, where he was born on January 7, 1961. Nestled in the heart of the state, Murdo was a quintessential small-town community that reflected the values of hard work, resilience, and close-knit relationships. These values would profoundly shape Thune's character and guide his future endeavors.

Growing up in Murdo, Thune was part of a family that prioritized service, faith, and education. His parents, Harold and Yvonne Thune, were pillars of the community. Harold, a World War II pilot, brought a sense of discipline and determination to the family. His experiences in the military taught him the importance of leadership and sacrifice, qualities he imparted to his children. Yvonne, on the other hand, nurtured the family with compassion and a strong moral compass, ensuring that her children were grounded in their values. John was the youngest of five siblings, and his childhood was marked by a blend of responsibility and opportunity.

In Murdo, everyone contributed to the community in some way, and the Thune family was no exception. Whether it was helping neighbors, attending church events, or participating in school activities, John was raised to appreciate the importance of contributing to the greater good. Education was a cornerstone of the Thune household. Harold and Yvonne instilled in their children the belief that learning was not just a pathway to success but a tool for making a positive impact on the world.

This belief resonated deeply with John, who excelled academically and demonstrated a curiosity for understanding the world beyond Murdo. A defining moment in Thune's early life occurred during a high school basketball game. As an athlete, he was passionate about sports, particularly basketball and track, which provided him with discipline and teamwork skills. At one of these games, Thune had the opportunity to meet U.S. Congressman Jim Abdnor, a fellow South Dakotan and a rising political figure. This chance encounter proved pivotal. Abdnor's genuine interest in Thune and his peers, coupled with his ability to connect with people from all walks of life, left a lasting impression.

For the young Thune, meeting Abdnor was more than just a fleeting moment; it was an awakening. He saw firsthand how a leader could inspire and uplift others while remaining approachable and grounded. This interaction planted the seed of a political aspiration, sparking a dream that would eventually lead him to Capitol Hill.

Building a Foundation Through Education

Following his high school graduation, Thune pursued higher education with the same determination that defined his earlier years. He enrolled at Biola University in La Mirada, California, where he earned a bachelor's degree in business administration. Biola, a private Christian university, provided him not only with academic rigor but also with an environment that reinforced his faith and ethical principles. At Biola, Thune developed a keen understanding of the intersection between business and public policy. He excelled in his studies, gaining insights into the economic principles that would later inform his political positions.

More importantly, his time at Biola broadened his perspective, exposing him to diverse ideas and experiences that enriched his worldview. Thune's commitment to education did not end with his undergraduate degree. Recognizing the value of advanced training in leadership and management, he pursued a Master of Business Administration (MBA) at the University of South Dakota.

This decision reflected his desire to deepen his expertise and prepare for a career that would demand both strategic thinking and practical problem-solving skills. During his MBA studies, Thune focused on the economic challenges facing rural communities like Murdo. His coursework often revolved around finding solutions to issues such as limited access to resources, infrastructure development, and economic diversification. These academic endeavors were more than theoretical exercises; they were deeply personal, rooted in his experiences growing up in a small town.

Shaping a Vision for the Future

Thune's educational journey was not solely about academics. His experiences during these formative years helped him crystallize a vision for his future. At Biola and the University of South Dakota, he encountered mentors and peers who challenged him to think critically about the role of government, the importance of ethical leadership, and the impact of public policy on everyday lives.

These experiences laid the groundwork for Thune's approach to politics. He began to see leadership not merely as a position of authority but as a responsibility to serve and uplift others. This philosophy would become a hallmark of his career, influencing his decisions and actions in every role he assumed. After completing his MBA, Thune returned to South Dakota, carrying with him the knowledge and skills he had acquired. His decision to come back was a testament to his enduring connection to his home state and his commitment to its people.

Unlike many who might have been drawn to opportunities in larger cities, Thune was determined to use his education to make a difference in the place that had shaped him. This return to his roots marked the beginning of Thune's journey into public service.

It was a period of reflection and preparation, during which he began to lay the foundation for a career that would bridge the aspirations of South Dakotans with the broader challenges of national governance. John Thune's early life and education set the stage for a remarkable career in politics. From his humble beginnings in Murdo to his academic achievements and formative experiences, every chapter of his early years contributed to the leader he would become. These years were not merely a prelude to his political journey but an integral part of the story, shaping his values, vision, and determination.

Chapter Two: Background

John Thune's background is deeply intertwined with the rich cultural and historical tapestry of South Dakota, a state known for its vast prairies, resilient communities, and enduring traditions. Born and raised in Murdo, a small town with a population of just a few hundred, Thune's upbringing was shaped by the values of hard work, perseverance, and service to others.

These principles were not only instilled in him by his family but also reinforced by the tight-knit community around him. Murdo, located in Jones County, epitomized the essence of rural America in the mid-20th century. Life in the town revolved around agriculture, small businesses, and communal activities. The people of Murdo valued honesty, dependability, and a strong work ethic—qualities that would come to define Thune's character and approach to leadership. Growing up in such an environment provided him with an intimate understanding of the challenges faced by rural communities, an awareness that would later influence his political priorities.

The Thune Family Legacy

The Thune family's roots in South Dakota run deep. Harold Thune, John's father, was a figure of both discipline and inspiration. A decorated World War II pilot, Harold exemplified courage and resilience, qualities he sought to pass on to his children. After the war, Harold returned to Murdo, where he became a schoolteacher, basketball coach, and an influential community leader. His dedication to service, both in the military and in civilian life, served as a powerful example for young John.

Yvonne Thune, John's mother, played an equally significant role in shaping his character. Known for her kindness and unwavering moral integrity, Yvonne was the heart of the Thune household. She ensured that her children were raised with a strong sense of right and wrong, teaching them the importance of empathy, faith, and perseverance. The Thunes were active members of their local church, and faith played a central role in their lives. For John, these early experiences in the church community fostered a sense of purpose and reinforced the idea that leadership should be guided by service to others.

Life in Murdo

Life in Murdo during Thune's childhood was marked by simplicity and a sense of shared responsibility. The town's small size meant that everyone knew one another, and neighbors often relied on each other for support. This close-knit environment taught Thune the value of community and the importance of working collaboratively to achieve common goals.

Murdo's economy was primarily agricultural, with many families, including the Thunes, involved in farming and related activities. From an early age, John understood the importance of hard work. Whether helping his family or contributing to local initiatives, he learned that success was often the result of perseverance and teamwork. Despite the town's modest resources, Murdo offered its residents a wealth of opportunities for personal and communal growth. Schools played a pivotal role in the community, not only as centers of learning but also as hubs for sports, music, and other extracurricular activities.

Thune was an active participant in these programs, excelling as an athlete while also developing his leadership skills.Beyond Murdo, South Dakota as a whole played a crucial role in shaping Thune's worldview. The state's vast landscapes and sparsely populated areas fostered a culture of self-reliance and innovation.

South Dakotans took pride in their ability to overcome challenges, whether those challenges came in the form of economic hardships or harsh winters. Politically, South Dakota was a state with a deep respect for individual freedoms and limited government intervention. These values resonated with Thune and would later influence his conservative philosophy. At the same time, the state's reliance on agriculture and small businesses highlighted the importance of policies that supported rural development and economic sustainability. As Thune grew older, he became increasingly aware of the unique needs of South Dakotans.

He observed how federal policies impacted local communities and began to develop a sense of how effective leadership could make a tangible difference. These observations would serve as the foundation for his eventual political platform, which emphasized the importance of representing the voices of rural America.

The Role of Mentorship and Community Leaders

While Thune's family played a central role in shaping his character, his broader community also provided numerous role models and mentors. Teachers, coaches, and local leaders in Murdo all contributed to his development, offering guidance and encouragement as he navigated his formative years. One of the most significant influences was Jim Abdnor, the U.S. Congressman from South Dakota whom Thune met during a high school basketball game. Abdnor's humility and dedication to public service left a lasting impression on Thune, inspiring him to consider a career in politics. The mentorship he later received from Abdnor during his early professional years was instrumental in preparing him for the challenges of leadership.

John Thune's background provided him with a solid foundation for his future endeavors. The lessons he learned in Murdo—about the importance of hard work, the value of community, and the power of perseverance—would guide him throughout his life. His upbringing instilled in him a deep respect for the people of South Dakota and a commitment to representing their interests on the national stage.

In many ways, Thune's background is a testament to the strength and resilience of rural America. It is a story of how the values of a small town can shape a leader who goes on to make a significant impact on the national and even global stage. Thune's journey from Murdo to the U.S. Senate is not just a reflection of his individual determination but also a celebration of the community that nurtured him and the principles that continue to guide him. This chapter captures the essence of Thune's roots, offering a glimpse into the experiences and values that shaped his character and leadership style. Let me know if you'd like to make any changes or approve this chapter before proceeding to the next.

Chapter Three: Academic Achievements

John Thune's academic journey was pivotal in shaping his intellectual foundation, leadership skills, and approach to problem-solving. From the small classrooms of Murdo to the esteemed halls of Biola University and the University of South Dakota, Thune's educational path reflects a steadfast commitment to learning and personal growth.

His academic achievements not only prepared him for the challenges of public service but also reinforced his belief in the transformative power of education. Thune's academic path began in the modest yet nurturing schools of Murdo, where education was valued as both a necessity and an opportunity. In the rural setting of Jones County, schools were central to the community, serving as hubs of learning, culture, and civic engagement. The teachers, often doubling as mentors and community leaders, played a critical role in guiding students toward their potential.

As a student, Thune demonstrated a natural aptitude for learning, coupled with a curiosity about the world beyond his hometown. He excelled in subjects like history and government, showcasing an early interest in understanding how societies functioned and how leadership could influence outcomes. His academic performance was matched by his participation in sports and extracurricular activities, which taught him discipline, teamwork, and the importance of balancing multiple responsibilities.

Biola University: A Broader Perspective

After graduating high school, Thune sought opportunities that would expand his horizons while remaining true to his values. In pursuit of higher education, he enrolled at Biola University in La Mirada, California. Known for its strong emphasis on Christian ethics and academic excellence, Biola provided Thune with an environment that aligned with his upbringing and aspirations. At Biola, Thune majored in business administration, a field that combined his interest in practical problem-solving with a desire to understand economic systems.

His coursework exposed him to subjects like finance, marketing, and organizational management, equipping him with skills that would later prove invaluable in both public and private sectors. Beyond academics, Biola was instrumental in broadening Thune's worldview. The university's diverse community introduced him to new perspectives, while its faith-based approach reinforced his commitment to integrity and service.

Thune's experiences at Biola laid the groundwork for his leadership philosophy, emphasizing the importance of ethical decision-making and responsibility to others. Eager to deepen his expertise and prepare for a future in leadership, Thune pursued a Master of Business Administration (MBA) at the University of South Dakota (USD). Returning to his home state for graduate studies reflected his enduring connection to South Dakota and his commitment to addressing the unique challenges faced by its communities. The MBA program at USD offered Thune an opportunity to refine his analytical skills and explore complex issues through a practical lens.

His studies focused on areas like economic development, rural policy, and strategic planning, all of which aligned with his growing interest in public service. During his time at USD, Thune distinguished himself as a dedicated and insightful student. His ability to connect theoretical knowledge with real-world applications set him apart, earning him the respect of his professors and peers. Through group projects, case studies, and internships,

He honed his ability to collaborate effectively and lead diverse teams. Thune's academic achievements were more than just milestones; they were stepping stones toward a greater purpose. At both Biola and USD, he encountered mentors and experiences that challenged him to think critically about the role of leadership in society. These moments of reflection helped him develop a vision for public service centered on accountability, innovation, and compassion. One defining aspect of Thune's education was his focus on the intersection of economics and governance.

He recognized that effective leadership required not only a deep understanding of policy but also an ability to navigate financial complexities and make data-driven decisions. This dual emphasis on policy and practicality would become a hallmark of his political career.

The Influence of Education on Leadership

Thune's academic background has had a lasting impact on his approach to leadership. His time at Biola instilled in him a sense of purpose and ethical responsibility, while his studies at USD equipped him with the tools to tackle complex challenges. Together, these experiences shaped a leader who is both principled and pragmatic, capable of addressing the needs of his constituents while navigating the intricacies of national governance. Throughout his career, Thune has often credited his education as a key factor in his success. He has emphasized the importance of lifelong learning, not only for personal growth but also for adapting to the evolving demands of leadership. His academic achievements serve as a testament to the power of education to transform lives and inspire action.

A Legacy Rooted in Learning

John Thune's academic journey is a story of ambition, perseverance, and purpose. From the classrooms of Murdo to the lecture halls of Biola and USD, his commitment to learning has been unwavering. These experiences laid the foundation for a career that would bridge the aspirations of South Dakotans with the broader challenges of national governance. This chapter captures the essence of Thune's educational achievements, offering insight into the experiences that shaped his intellect and leadership style. Let me know if you'd like to make any changes or approve this chapter before proceeding to the next.

Chapter Four: Personal Experience

John Thune's life has been shaped by a wealth of personal experiences that have informed his character, leadership style, and approach to public service. From his formative years in Murdo to his time in Washington, D.C., these moments have provided him with insights and lessons that extend beyond formal education or professional roles.

Each experience has contributed to his sense of purpose, his ability to connect with others, and his unwavering commitment to serving his constituents. Thune's early years in the rural setting of Murdo, South Dakota, were foundational to his personal growth. Life in a small town demanded resilience, adaptability, and a strong sense of community. Murdo's close-knit environment encouraged Thune to value relationships, recognize the importance of collective effort, and appreciate the everyday struggles of ordinary citizens. Growing up in a household led by Harold and Yvonne Thune, John was exposed to values that would guide him throughout his life.

Harold's discipline as a World War II pilot and basketball coach introduced Thune to the importance of focus, perseverance, and leading by example. Meanwhile, Yvonne's nurturing nature and moral integrity instilled in him a sense of compassion and a deep respect for others. Thune's participation in sports further shaped his character. As a high school basketball player, he learned the importance of teamwork, discipline, and handling both victory and defeat with grace.

Sports also provided him with an outlet for leadership, as he often took on roles that required him to motivate and guide his teammates. One of the most defining personal experiences in Thune's early life was his chance meeting with Congressman Jim Abdnor. This encounter, which occurred at a high school basketball game, left a lasting impression on the young Thune. Abdnor's genuine interest in the lives of his constituents and his ability to connect with people on a personal level inspired Thune to consider a career in public service. This moment wasn't just a fleeting interaction; it was a catalyst for Thune's political aspirations.

It demonstrated to him the profound impact that accessible and empathetic leadership could have on individuals and communities. This experience would later guide his approach to representing South Dakotans, emphasizing personal connection and attentiveness to their needs.

Early Professional Challenges and Growth

After completing his MBA at the University of South Dakota, Thune embarked on a career that allowed him to blend his academic knowledge with real-world applications. His early roles, including working for Congressman Abdnor and the Small Business Administration during the Reagan administration, exposed him to the complexities of governance and policy making. These positions were not without their challenges. Navigating the intricacies of federal bureaucracy and addressing the diverse needs of constituents required Thune to develop resilience and problem-solving skills. These experiences also reinforced the importance of balancing long-term vision with immediate action, a principle that would become central to his leadership style.

Family Life and its Impact on Leadership

Thune's personal life has been a source of strength and perspective throughout his career. His marriage to Kimberley Weems has provided him with a partner who shares his values and commitment to family and community. Together, they have raised two daughters, fostering a household that emphasizes faith, mutual respect, and a sense of purpose.

As a father, Thune has drawn on his own upbringing to guide his children, instilling in them the values of integrity, hard work, and service. His experiences as a husband and father have also influenced his approach to leadership, reminding him of the importance of policies that support families and strengthen communities. Thune's family has been an integral part of his public life. Kimberley's support and involvement in community initiatives have complemented Thune's efforts, creating a partnership that extends beyond the personal into the public realm. Their shared commitment to faith and service has reinforced Thune's belief in leading by example.

Throughout his life, Thune's faith has been a cornerstone of his personal and professional journey. Raised in a devout Christian household, he has consistently drawn on his spiritual beliefs to navigate challenges and make decisions. Faith has provided him with a sense of purpose and a moral framework that guides his interactions with others. In public service, Thune's faith has translated into a leadership style that prioritizes empathy, humility, and accountability.

He has often spoken about the importance of aligning actions with values, emphasizing that true leadership involves serving others with integrity and respect. Despite his success on the national stage, Thune has remained deeply connected to his roots in South Dakota. His personal experiences in the state, from growing up in Murdo to representing its residents in Congress, have kept him grounded. Thune frequently returns to South Dakota, engaging with constituents and participating in local events to stay attuned to the needs and aspirations of the people he serves.

These connections are not merely symbolic; they are central to Thune's leadership philosophy. He has often emphasized the importance of understanding the everyday experiences of constituents, recognizing that effective governance begins with listening and responding to their concerns.

Personal Growth Through Challenges

Thune's journey has not been without obstacles. Whether navigating political setbacks or facing the pressures of public life, he has consistently approached challenges as opportunities for growth. His ability to remain composed and focused during difficult times has earned him respect from colleagues and constituents alike. These experiences have also shaped his perspective on resilience and perseverance. Thune's ability to adapt to changing circumstances and maintain his commitment to his values underscores his dedication to serving others with integrity.

John Thune's personal experiences have been instrumental in shaping his approach to public service. From his early years in Murdo to his current role as a U.S. senator, these moments have provided him with insights into the power of community, the importance of empathy, and the value of perseverance. This chapter highlights the human side of Thune's journey, offering a glimpse into the experiences that have shaped his character and leadership style. Let me know if you'd like to make any changes or approve this chapter before proceeding to the next.

Chapter Five: Early Career

John Thune's early career marked the beginning of a journey defined by dedication, hard work, and a growing passion for public service. These formative years were critical in shaping his skills, values, and political philosophy. His experiences during this period laid a strong foundation for his future in leadership and governance, as he transitioned from academic pursuits to roles that would immerse him in the intricacies of policy making and public administration.

Working with Jim Abdnor: A Transformative Start

Thune's first major professional experience began under the mentorship of Congressman Jim Abdnor, a figure who had been a source of inspiration since their initial meeting during Thune's high school years. Joining Abdnor's team as a legislative assistant provided Thune with an insider's view of the workings of Congress. Based in Washington, D.C., Thune's responsibilities included researching policy issues, drafting legislation, and engaging with constituents on behalf of Abdnor's office.

These tasks required not only analytical skills but also a keen understanding of how national policies impacted South Dakota's communities. This role was a crash course in the realities of federal governance, offering Thune invaluable lessons in diplomacy, negotiation, and the importance of addressing constituent needs. Abdnor's leadership style left a lasting impression on Thune. Known for his humility and accessibility, Abdnor modeled a form of leadership that prioritized service over self-interest.

Thune carried these lessons forward, integrating them into his own approach to public service. After his tenure with Abdnor, Thune took on a role at the Small Business Administration (SBA) during President Ronald Reagan's administration. As a liaison for the agency, Thune worked on initiatives aimed at supporting small businesses across the United States. This role exposed him to the challenges faced by entrepreneurs and small business owners, particularly in rural areas like South Dakota. He gained firsthand experience in crafting policies that aimed to stimulate economic growth, foster innovation, and reduce bureaucratic obstacles for small businesses.

Thune's time at the SBA deepened his understanding of the relationship between federal policies and local economies. It also reinforced his belief in the importance of empowering individuals and communities through economic opportunity, a theme that would later become central to his political agenda.

Return to South Dakota: State-Level Engagement

Following his work in Washington, Thune returned to South Dakota, bringing with him a wealth of experience and a renewed commitment to serving his home state. He took on leadership roles at various organizations, including the South Dakota Republican Party, where he worked to strengthen the party's presence and support local candidates. During this period, Thune also served as the executive director of the South Dakota Municipal League, an organization focused on advocating for the interests of local governments. This role provided him with a deeper understanding of the challenges faced by city officials and municipal leaders, ranging from infrastructure development to budgetary constraints.

Through his engagement with state and local leaders, Thune developed a nuanced perspective on governance, recognizing the importance of collaboration between different levels of government. These experiences solidified his reputation as a dedicated advocate for South Dakota's communities. Thune's early career successes did not go unnoticed. His work ethic, ability to connect with people, and growing expertise in public policy positioned him as a rising star within the Republican Party.

Encouraged by mentors and colleagues, Thune began to consider running for public office himself. The decision to enter the political arena was not made lightly. Thune recognized the demands and sacrifices associated with public service, as well as the potential impact he could have on South Dakota and the nation. Ultimately, his desire to make a difference outweighed any reservations, and he embarked on his first campaign with a determination to bring positive change to his constituents. Thune's early career experiences were instrumental in shaping his leadership style, which is characterized by a blend of pragmatism, empathy, and a commitment to ethical governance.

Whether working on Capitol Hill, advocating for small businesses, or engaging with local governments, he consistently prioritized listening to and addressing the needs of the people he served. These roles also taught him the importance of resilience and adaptability. In the fast-paced world of politics and public administration, challenges were inevitable. Thune's ability to remain focused and composed, even in the face of adversity, became one of his defining traits as a leader.

Building Relationships and Networks

Throughout his early career, Thune placed a strong emphasis on building relationships and fostering collaboration. He recognized that effective leadership required not only individual effort but also the ability to work with diverse groups of people, including colleagues, constituents, and stakeholders. His network of mentors and allies, including figures like Jim Abdnor, provided guidance and support as he navigated the complexities of public service. At the same time, Thune's approachable demeanor and genuine interest in others earned him the trust and respect of those he worked with.

Thune's early career was a period of growth, learning, and preparation for the challenges that lay ahead. It reinforced key principles that would guide him throughout his life, including the importance of humility, perseverance, and a focus on service over self-interest. These formative experiences also provided him with a deep understanding of the issues facing South Dakota and the nation, from economic development to the needs of rural communities.

This knowledge, combined with his natural leadership abilities, set the stage for his eventual rise to elected office. John Thune's early career was more than just a series of professional roles; it was the foundation of a political legacy rooted in service, integrity, and a commitment to the people of South Dakota. Each experience contributed to his development as a leader, equipping him with the skills and values needed to navigate the challenges of public life. This chapter captures the essence of Thune's early career, highlighting the moments that shaped his journey and prepared him for the responsibilities of leadership. Let me know if you'd like to make any changes or approve this chapter before proceeding to the next.

Chapter Six: Political Journey

John Thune's political journey is a testament to his resilience, vision, and dedication to public service. From his initial foray into politics as a congressional aide to his rise as one of the most respected leaders in the U.S. Senate, Thune's career reflects his unwavering commitment to South Dakota and the nation. This chapter delves into the pivotal moments that defined his political path and explores how his values and experiences shaped his approach to governance.

A Humble Beginning in Public Service

Thune's political career began modestly, working behind the scenes in the office of Congressman Jim Abdnor. As a legislative aide, he was immersed in the intricacies of policymaking, learning the ropes of legislative processes and constituent engagement. This experience allowed Thune to observe firsthand the impact of thoughtful leadership and effective communication. Abdnor's mentorship left an indelible mark on Thune, instilling in him a sense of duty and a focus on addressing the practical needs of constituents.

These lessons would serve as guiding principles throughout his career, influencing his approach to problem-solving and policymaking. In 1996, Thune decided to run for South Dakota's At-Large Congressional District in the U.S. House of Representatives. The decision marked a significant turning point in his life, transitioning from a behind-the-scenes role to one where he would be directly accountable to voters.

Thune's campaign was rooted in his deep connection to South Dakota and his understanding of the state's unique challenges. He focused on issues such as economic development, agriculture, and education, emphasizing his commitment to improving the lives of his constituents. His grassroots approach resonated with voters, and he won the election, beginning his tenure in the U.S. House. Over the next six years, Thune established himself as a dedicated representative, advocating for policies that supported rural communities, strengthened local economies, and enhanced opportunities for South Dakotans.

After serving three terms in the House, Thune set his sights on the U.S. Senate. In 2002, he challenged incumbent Senator Tim Johnson in a closely watched race. Despite a strong campaign, Thune narrowly lost, a defeat that tested his resilience and determination. Rather than retreating from public life, Thune used the experience as an opportunity for growth.

He reflected on the lessons learned from the campaign, refined his strategy, and deepened his connection with South Dakota voters. In 2004, Thune ran for the Senate again, this time challenging Senate Minority Leader Tom Daschle. The race was one of the most intense and high-profile contests in the nation, drawing significant attention from both parties. Thune's message of change and his focus on issues that mattered most to South Dakotans ultimately resonated, and he won the election, unseating Daschle and beginning his tenure as a U.S. senator.

Establishing a Reputation in the Senate

As a senator, Thune quickly established himself as a pragmatic and effective legislator. He focused on building relationships with colleagues across the political spectrum, earning a reputation as a consensus-builder and a problem-solver. Thune's legislative priorities reflected his commitment to South Dakota's interests and the broader needs of the nation. He played a key role in advancing policies related to agriculture, energy, and tax reform, leveraging his position on influential committees to advocate for meaningful change.

Over time, Thune's leadership abilities earned him recognition within the Senate Republican Conference. He held several leadership positions, including chairman of the Senate Republican Policy Committee and chairman of the Senate Commerce, Science, and Transportation Committee. In these roles, Thune was instrumental in shaping the Republican legislative agenda, focusing on issues such as infrastructure development, regulatory reform, and technological innovation. His ability to articulate complex policies in a clear and accessible manner made him a trusted voice among his colleagues and constituents alike.

In 2019, Thune was elected Senate Minority Whip, the second-highest-ranking position in the Republican Conference. This role further cemented his influence within the party, allowing him to play a key role in strategic decision-making and legislative negotiations.

The Road to Majority Leader

Thune's political journey reached a new milestone in 2025 when he was elected Senate Majority Leader, succeeding Mitch McConnell. This achievement reflected the trust and respect he had earned from his colleagues over decades of service. As Majority Leader, Thune faced the challenge of navigating a deeply divided political landscape. He emphasized the importance of bipartisanship, seeking common ground on critical issues while remaining true to his conservative principles. Thune's leadership style as Majority Leader was characterized by a focus on collaboration, transparency, and accountability. He worked to ensure that the Senate remained a forum for meaningful debate and effective governance, balancing the demands of his party with the broader needs of the nation.

John Thune's political journey is a story of perseverance, growth, and impact. From his early days as a congressional aide to his current role as Senate Majority Leader, he has consistently demonstrated a commitment to serving the people of South Dakota and the United States.

Throughout his career, Thune has remained grounded in his values, prioritizing integrity, empathy, and a focus on results. His ability to navigate challenges with grace and determination has earned him the respect of colleagues and constituents alike, solidifying his legacy as one of the most influential leaders of his generation. This chapter highlights the key milestones and defining moments of Thune's political journey. Let me know if you'd like to make any changes or approve this chapter before proceeding to the next.

Chapter seven: Political Career

John Thune's political career is distinguished by his ability to merge policy expertise with a steadfast commitment to public service. His tenure in public office reflects a focus on delivering results for his constituents, navigating complex political dynamics, and shaping legislative priorities at both the national and local levels. This chapter delves into the defining aspects of his political career, emphasizing his time in the U.S. House of Representatives, his transformative years in the Senate, and his influence on the Republican Party.

U.S. House of Representatives: 1997–2003

John Thune's journey into elected office began in 1996 when he won South Dakota's At-Large Congressional District seat in the U.S. House of Representatives. During his three terms, Thune's work was characterized by a deep understanding of his state's unique needs and a commitment to addressing them through effective policy-making. As a congressman, Thune became a vocal advocate for agricultural reform, recognizing the central role that farming and ranching played in South Dakota's economy.

He worked on legislation aimed at providing financial support to struggling farmers, expanding access to markets, and ensuring fair trade policies that benefited American agriculture. Thune also prioritized education, seeking to improve funding for rural schools and championing programs that increased access to higher education for South Dakota's youth.

His efforts to bridge the digital divide by promoting broadband access in underserved areas demonstrated his forward-thinking approach to economic development. Beyond policy, Thune gained a reputation for his accessibility and responsiveness to constituents. He frequently traveled across the state, holding town hall meetings and engaging with South Dakotans on the ground. This hands-on approach not only strengthened his connection with voters but also ensured that his legislative priorities were directly informed by their concerns. After deciding not to seek re-election in 2002 to challenge Senator Tim Johnson, Thune experienced a narrow and disappointing loss.

However, his resilience and determination set the stage for his return to politics. In 2004, Thune made history by unseating Senate Minority Leader Tom Daschle, a feat that underscored his political acumen and ability to galvanize support. Thune's tenure in the Senate has been marked by his influence on key legislative initiatives and his ascent to prominent leadership roles.

Legislative Achievements

As a senator, Thune focused on issues central to South Dakota and the nation. His work on agricultural policy continued, with efforts to modernize the Farm Bill and ensure that rural communities received the support they needed. He championed renewable energy initiatives, particularly the development of biofuels and wind energy, aligning economic growth with environmental sustainability. Thune was also instrumental in tax reform efforts, playing a key role in the passage of legislation aimed at reducing the tax burden on individuals and businesses. His expertise in financial policy earned him a seat on the Senate Finance Committee, where he worked to craft solutions that balanced fiscal responsibility with economic opportunity.

Thune's ability to build consensus and navigate the complexities of the legislative process earned him recognition as a natural leader. He held several influential positions within the Senate Republican Conference, including chairman of the Republican Policy Committee and chairman of the Senate Commerce, Science, and Transportation Committee.

In these roles, Thune shaped the party's policy agenda, focusing on infrastructure development, technological innovation, and deregulation. His efforts to foster bipartisanship in areas such as transportation and telecommunications legislation demonstrated his commitment to achieving tangible results for the American people. In 2019, Thune's leadership trajectory reached new heights when he was elected Senate Minority Whip, the second-highest position in the Republican caucus. His responsibilities included coordinating legislative strategies, rallying party support, and serving as a key advisor to the Minority Leader.

Majority Leader: A New Era of Leadership

In January 2025, Thune was elected Senate Majority Leader, succeeding Mitch McConnell. This position marked the culmination of decades of public service and highlighted the trust and respect he had garnered within the Senate. As Majority Leader, Thune faced the challenge of leading the Senate during a period of intense political polarization. He emphasized the importance of restoring civility and bipartisanship, working to find common ground on issues such as infrastructure, healthcare, and national security.

Thune's leadership style was defined by his pragmatism and focus on results. He sought to balance the demands of his party with the broader interests of the nation, ensuring that the Senate remained a platform for meaningful debate and effective governance. Throughout his political career, Thune has been a steady and influential voice within the Republican Party. His focus on fiscal conservatism, limited government, and individual liberty aligned with core Republican principles, while his willingness to engage with opposing viewpoints demonstrated a commitment to collaborative governance.

Thune's ability to articulate the party's vision and priorities in a clear and compelling manner made him a valuable spokesperson and a trusted leader. His work to modernize the party's approach to issues such as technology and energy reflected his forward-looking perspective and adaptability to changing times. John Thune's political career is a testament to the power of perseverance, integrity, and a deep commitment to public service. From his early days in the U.S. House to his leadership in the Senate, Thune has consistently demonstrated a focus on delivering results for his constituents and advancing policies that promote growth, opportunity, and fairness.

Chapter Eight : Net Worth

John Thune's financial journey provides insight into his prudent management of personal assets, reflective of his Midwestern values of frugality and responsibility. Over the years, Thune's net worth has been shaped by his earnings as a public servant, prudent investments, and his adherence to a lifestyle rooted in modesty.

Early Financial Foundation

Thune's financial outlook was shaped by his upbringing in Murdo, South Dakota, a small town where resourcefulness was a way of life. Growing up in a family that valued hard work and practicality, Thune developed an early appreciation for financial discipline. His academic pursuits, including a business administration degree and an MBA, further refined his understanding of economics and personal finance, equipping him with the tools to make sound financial decisions. A significant portion of Thune's net worth stems from his salary as a public servant. Beginning with his time as a legislative aide and later as an executive director of the South Dakota Municipal League,

Thune's early roles provided stable income while also grounding him in the realities of fiscal responsibility in public administration. His service in the U.S. House of Representatives (1997–2003) and the U.S. Senate (2005–present) has been accompanied by congressional salaries, which are regulated and transparent. As of 2024, the annual salary for a U.S. senator is approximately $174,000. While this income is significant, Thune has consistently emphasized his commitment to serving the public rather than personal financial gain.

Thune's financial portfolio reflects his cautious and calculated approach to wealth management. His investments are largely diversified, with holdings in mutual funds, retirement accounts, and other financial instruments designed for steady growth rather than high-risk ventures. Unlike many politicians, Thune has avoided entanglements in speculative investments or high-profile financial ventures, choosing instead to prioritize stability and sustainability. This approach aligns with his personal values and his understanding of the long-term importance of financial security. Thune's primary real estate asset is his family home in Sioux Falls, South Dakota.

The property, modest yet comfortable, underscores his preference for a grounded lifestyle that aligns with his constituents' values. His choice to reside in Sioux Falls highlights his connection to his roots and his desire to maintain a presence in the community he represents. Additionally, Thune has owned other modest properties over the years, often tied to his work in Washington, D.C., and his need for proximity to the Capitol.

These properties have typically been practical in nature, serving his professional needs rather than acting as investments or symbols of affluence. One of the defining characteristics of Thune's financial profile is his commitment to living within his means. Despite his position as a high-ranking senator, Thune's lifestyle is notably understated, reflecting his Midwestern sensibilities. Thune has often spoken about the importance of fiscal responsibility, both in personal finance and public governance. His own financial practices mirror this philosophy, emphasizing the importance of budgeting, saving, and avoiding unnecessary extravagance.

Wealth Transparency and Ethics

As a public servant, Thune is required to file annual financial disclosure reports, providing transparency about his assets, liabilities, and sources of income. These reports have consistently demonstrated his adherence to ethical standards and his commitment to avoiding conflicts of interest. Thune's financial disclosures reveal a careful separation between his personal wealth and his responsibilities as a senator.

He has avoided investments in industries or entities that could pose ethical dilemmas, prioritizing the integrity of his public service over personal financial gain. While not a primary driver of his net worth, Thune's commitment to philanthropy is an important aspect of his financial story. He and his family have supported various charitable causes, particularly those focused on education, community development, and support for veterans. Thune's giving reflects his belief in the power of community and his desire to use his resources to make a positive impact. This commitment to giving back aligns with his broader values of service and responsibility.

In the context of his peers in Congress, Thune's net worth is relatively modest. While some members of Congress boast significant personal wealth from business ventures or inheritances, Thune's financial profile is rooted in earned income and prudent investments. This distinction reinforces his reputation as a leader who remains connected to the experiences of everyday Americans.

A Financial Legacy of Integrity

John Thune's net worth is not merely a reflection of his financial assets but also a testament to his character and values. His approach to wealth management emphasizes responsibility, transparency, and a focus on long-term stability over short-term gain. As he continues to serve in public office, Thune's financial practices remain an integral part of his broader legacy. They underscore his commitment to ethical leadership, his respect for the trust placed in him by his constituents, and his dedication to living by the principles he espouses. This chapter highlights the facets of Thune's financial journey and his approach to balancing personal wealth with public service. Let me know if you'd like any revisions or approve this chapter before moving to the next.

Chapter Nine: Legacy and Influence

John Thune's legacy extends far beyond his tenure in office. His influence on both South Dakota and national politics is deeply felt through his leadership, legislative accomplishments, and commitment to public service. Throughout his career, Thune has been a driving force in shaping the Republican Party's platform, advancing policies that resonate with conservative values, and fostering a political environment grounded in integrity and pragmatism.

In this chapter, we explore Thune's enduring legacy and the lasting impact he has had on American politics, both as a policymaker and as a public servant. Thune's legacy is deeply intertwined with the state of South Dakota, where his influence as both a congressman and a senator has been transformative. Throughout his political career, Thune's work has been guided by a steadfast commitment to addressing the unique challenges and opportunities facing his home state. One of Thune's most significant contributions has been his advocacy for South Dakota's agricultural community.

Agriculture has long been the backbone of the state's economy, and Thune has used his platform in Congress and the Senate to fight for policies that support farmers, ranchers, and rural communities. His efforts to reform farm programs, secure trade agreements that benefit American agriculture, and provide disaster relief have been key to bolstering the sector. In addition to agriculture, Thune has focused on expanding access to technology and infrastructure in South Dakota.

He was an early advocate for expanding broadband internet to rural areas, ensuring that underserved communities have the same access to information and opportunities as urban counterparts. His efforts to modernize South Dakota's infrastructure, particularly in transportation and energy, have helped the state grow and remain competitive in a rapidly changing global economy. Thune's deep connection to South Dakota is also evident in his work on behalf of veterans, rural healthcare, and education. He has worked to secure funding for healthcare facilities that serve rural populations and has consistently advocated for policies that support the state's veterans, many of whom depend on federal benefits and support services.

His support for South Dakota's education system, including initiatives to improve funding for rural schools, has earned him the respect and trust of educators and parents across the state. Beyond South Dakota, Thune's influence in the Senate has been felt across the nation. His tenure as a U.S. senator has seen him take on pivotal roles in shaping national policy, particularly in areas such as tax reform, energy policy, and technological innovation.

Tax Reform and Economic Policy

Thune has been a tireless advocate for tax reform, particularly through his work on the Tax Cuts and Jobs Act of 2017. As a key player in the Senate's efforts to reform the U.S. tax code, Thune played an integral role in shaping the provisions that reduced corporate tax rates, simplified individual tax brackets, and expanded tax relief for families. His support for lowering the corporate tax rate was driven by his belief that it would spur job creation, economic growth, and increased competitiveness for U.S. businesses. In addition to his work on the 2017 tax reform, Thune has been a vocal proponent of reducing government spending and limiting the federal deficit.

He has consistently called for fiscal responsibility, emphasizing the need for a balanced budget and reforms that prioritize long-term economic sustainability. As chairman of the Senate Committee on Commerce, Science, and Transportation, Thune has had a significant impact on national energy policy. He has advocated for the development of renewable energy sources, particularly biofuels, which are a key part of South Dakota's energy sector.

His support for clean energy alternatives aligns with his belief in promoting energy independence while addressing environmental concerns. Thune has also played a role in the nation's infrastructure development, particularly in improving the nation's roads, bridges, and broadband networks. He has advocated for investment in both traditional and digital infrastructure, emphasizing the importance of a robust and modern infrastructure system for economic growth and national security. Thune's work on technology and innovation has also been notable. As the chairman of the Senate Commerce Committee, he has been at the forefront of issues related to the regulation of emerging technologies, including telecommunications, cybersecurity, and artificial intelligence.

His approach to these complex issues has been guided by a commitment to fostering innovation while balancing the need for privacy protections and national security. Thune has championed policies that encourage technological advancements, recognizing that technology plays a crucial role in the future of the American economy. His efforts to ensure that the U.S. remains competitive in the global technological landscape have cemented his reputation as a forward-thinking leader.

Influence Within the Republican Party

Thune's leadership within the Republican Party has been one of the defining aspects of his career. Known for his pragmatic, results-oriented approach, Thune has emerged as a key figure in shaping the party's direction, particularly in the areas of fiscal policy, national security, and social issues. His ability to build consensus among Republicans, as well as his willingness to engage with Democrats on critical issues, has earned him respect on both sides of the aisle. Thune's leadership has been instrumental in shaping the party's response to pressing issues such as healthcare reform, tax policy, and budgetary concerns.

In 2025, when Thune was elected Senate Majority Leader, his influence within the Republican Party reached new heights. As Majority Leader, Thune is poised to play a pivotal role in guiding the Senate through a period of political polarization, working to advance the party's agenda while maintaining the Senate's role as a deliberative body focused on bipartisan solutions. Thune's leadership style, which emphasizes collaboration and integrity, has set him apart from many of his contemporaries.

His ability to balance the interests of his party with the needs of the American people has positioned him as a respected and effective leader in the Senate. Thune's legacy is ultimately one of service and integrity. His long tenure in public office has been marked by a dedication to improving the lives of his constituents, advancing conservative values, and fostering a political culture based on respect, responsibility, and results. Through his work in the U.S. House and Senate, Thune has left a lasting imprint on the nation's policy landscape. His focus on economic growth, energy independence, and technological innovation has shaped the country's trajectory, and his efforts to modernize the Republican Party have helped position it for future challenges.

Beyond policy, Thune's legacy is also rooted in his unwavering commitment to ethical leadership. He has earned a reputation for honesty, transparency, and a focus on the greater good, setting an example for future generations of public servants. This chapter highlights the far-reaching impact of John Thune's political career and the lasting contributions he has made to both South Dakota and the United States. Let me know if you would like any revisions or approve this chapter before proceeding to the next.

Chapter Ten: Personal Life

John Thune's personal life is marked by his deep connection to his family, his love for his home state, and his commitment to maintaining a sense of normalcy despite the demands of public office. While his political career often places him in the public eye, Thune has worked hard to preserve a private and grounded personal life, one that reflects his values of humility, faith, and service to others.

Family Life and Marriage

At the heart of Thune's personal life is his family. He is married to Kimberley Weems, a former teacher, and together they have two daughters, Larissa and Brittany. Thune and Kimberley's relationship is a testament to their shared values of faith, hard work, and commitment to family. The couple's bond has been described as a partnership built on mutual respect and a shared desire to contribute positively to their community and the nation. Kimberley has been a steady and supportive presence throughout Thune's political career, balancing the demands of public life with raising their children and contributing to the family's charitable efforts.

Thune has often praised his wife for her strength and unwavering support, acknowledging that their family life is a source of grounding and stability amidst the fast-paced and often contentious world of politics. Their daughters, Larissa and Brittany, have been raised in Sioux Falls, where the family maintains a strong sense of connection to the community. Thune has spoken often about the importance of raising his children with a sense of humility and a focus on values rather than material wealth or fame.

The family enjoys a relatively private life in South Dakota, often attending local church services, participating in community events, and enjoying time outdoors. Faith plays a central role in Thune's life, guiding both his personal decisions and his political philosophy. Raised in a Christian household, Thune's religious convictions have been a cornerstone of his public and private life. He has openly spoken about the importance of his faith in shaping his worldview, his commitment to moral integrity, and his understanding of service to others. Thune's Christian faith has informed much of his political career, particularly in his stance on social issues such as marriage, family, and the sanctity of life.

He is known for his pro-life position and his advocacy for religious freedom, values that align with his personal belief system and his desire to protect the rights of individuals to live according to their faith. In addition to his faith, Thune places great emphasis on the importance of personal integrity, humility, and responsibility. These values are evident not only in his public service but also in how he conducts himself in his personal life.

Thune is often described as a man of principle, whose actions align with his words, and who remains deeply committed to maintaining a high standard of ethics and integrity. Despite his demanding career, Thune has a number of personal interests and hobbies that allow him to unwind and maintain a balanced life. His love for the outdoors is one of the defining aspects of his personal life. Growing up in rural South Dakota, Thune developed a strong connection to nature, and he continues to enjoy outdoor activities such as hiking, hunting, and fishing. Thune's passion for sports is also a central part of his life. In his younger years, he played basketball and was even encouraged to pursue a professional career in sports.

Although politics ultimately became his calling, Thune remains an avid sports fan, often attending local games and supporting South Dakota's athletic programs. His appreciation for teamwork and competition, combined with his belief in personal discipline and perseverance, has shaped both his professional and personal lives. In his free time, Thune enjoys reading, particularly on topics related to history, economics, and public policy.

His curiosity about the world and his desire to continually learn are key aspects of his personality, and they have influenced his approach to leadership and governance. Thune's commitment to his community extends beyond his political role. He and his family are deeply involved in charitable work, supporting a variety of causes in South Dakota and beyond. Thune has consistently advocated for the importance of giving back, particularly to organizations that focus on education, healthcare, veterans, and the less fortunate. Thune has been a strong proponent of programs that provide support to veterans, reflecting his respect and admiration for those who have served the nation.

His advocacy for veterans' issues is matched by his family's personal involvement in local veterans' organizations and events. Education has also been a key focus for Thune and his family. They have supported efforts to improve educational opportunities for children in South Dakota, particularly in underserved areas. Thune's emphasis on the importance of education aligns with his belief in the value of hard work and the need for every individual to have access to opportunities for growth and success.

Thune's involvement in community organizations, his support for local initiatives, and his dedication to service have earned him respect not only as a politician but as a committed member of his community. His personal life is marked by a deep sense of responsibility, and he works to ensure that his actions both in and out of the Senate reflect his commitment to making a positive difference in the lives of others. Despite his high-profile career, Thune has made a concerted effort to maintain his privacy and balance his public and private lives. He and his family have largely avoided the media spotlight, preferring a quiet and humble existence in Sioux Falls. Thune's ability to maintain a sense of normalcy in his personal life has been a key factor in his longevity in politics.

Thune has often remarked that his personal life is where he finds his true sense of purpose and peace. While his political career has been demanding, he finds solace in spending time with his family, attending church, and enjoying the simple pleasures of life in South Dakota. This balance has allowed him to remain grounded, even as he navigates the challenges of national politics.

John Thune's personal life offers a glimpse into the man behind the public figure. His commitment to family, faith, and community reflects the values that have guided his political career and personal choices. Thune's ability to maintain a private and balanced life, even amidst the demands of public office, has been a testament to his discipline and integrity. His personal life serves as a foundation for his success as a public servant and a reminder of the importance of staying true to one's values in both public and private spheres.

Chapter Eleven: Impact

John Thune's career in the U.S. Senate has been marked by a series of significant legislative achievements, a consistent commitment to conservative principles, and an ability to shape national policy in ways that reflect his vision for America. As he prepares to step into the role of Senate Majority Leader in 2025, his impact on American politics and the state of South Dakota remains substantial, with his influence spanning economic policy, national security, and social issues.

Economic Impact

One of Thune's most lasting contributions to the political landscape is his work on tax reform. As a staunch advocate for reducing the tax burden on businesses and individuals, Thune played a key role in the passage of the Tax Cuts and Jobs Act of 2017. This landmark legislation, which lowered corporate tax rates and provided tax cuts for individuals, had a significant effect on the U.S. economy. Thune's work in this area is not only remembered for his advocacy but also for his ability to build bipartisan support for policies that promote growth and job creation.

His economic philosophy centers on the belief that a free-market economy, supported by a fair tax system, is the key to America's prosperity. Thune's efforts to address economic challenges have also focused on policies aimed at supporting small businesses, farmers, and rural communities. Through his leadership, he has championed initiatives that expand broadband access in underserved areas, improve infrastructure, and enhance opportunities for agricultural development.

These contributions have particularly benefited his home state of South Dakota, where agriculture plays a central role in the economy. By advocating for policies that support the economic health of rural America, Thune has cemented his legacy as a champion for rural communities, ensuring that they receive the resources necessary to thrive in a rapidly changing world. Thune's influence on national security and foreign policy has also been significant. As a member of the Senate Armed Services Committee, he has been an outspoken advocate for the military and for policies that enhance the security of the United States.

Thune's work on defense spending, military readiness, and the protection of American interests abroad reflects his dedication to ensuring that the U.S. remains a global leader in both military and diplomatic affairs. Thune's support for veterans has been another key area of focus. He has worked tirelessly to improve the benefits and services provided to military veterans, ensuring they have access to the care and resources they deserve after their service.

His advocacy for veterans' issues has earned him the respect and admiration of both his colleagues in Congress and his constituents, particularly those who have served in the armed forces. In addition to his work on defense and veterans' issues, Thune has been an advocate for a robust foreign policy that prioritizes American interests while fostering strong relationships with key allies. His role in supporting policies to combat terrorism, safeguard democracy, and strengthen international partnerships has made him a key figure in shaping U.S. foreign policy in the post-9/11 world.

Social and Cultural Impact

Beyond economic and national security issues, Thune has also been a significant voice on social and cultural issues. A strong supporter of traditional values, Thune has consistently advocated for policies that reflect his conservative beliefs. His positions on issues such as marriage, the sanctity of life, and religious freedom have aligned with his faith-based worldview and have been central to his political platform.

Thune's stance on social issues has resonated with many Americans who share his commitment to preserving the moral fabric of the nation. Thune's work in the Senate also reflects his broader vision for American society—one that emphasizes personal responsibility, the importance of family, and the need for policies that foster a sense of community and national unity. His ability to address cultural challenges while upholding his values has made him a voice of reason in an increasingly polarized political environment. Thune's role in shaping public discourse on these issues has cemented his reputation as a leader who is not afraid to stand up for his beliefs, even when doing so may not be politically expedient.

Impact on South Dakota

Thune's impact on his home state of South Dakota cannot be overstated. From the moment he was first elected to the U.S. House in 1996, Thune has been a tireless advocate for South Dakota's interests in Washington. His work has benefited the state in a number of ways, from securing funding for infrastructure projects to advocating for policies that support the state's agricultural sector.

Thune's dedication to improving the lives of his constituents is evident in his support for rural broadband expansion, his efforts to protect agricultural subsidies, and his advocacy for policies that enhance the economic development of small towns and rural communities. His ability to navigate the complexities of federal policy while keeping South Dakota's unique needs at the forefront of his work has made him one of the state's most influential politicians in modern history. Moreover, Thune's ability to connect with his constituents and maintain strong ties to his home state has been a key factor in his political success.

He remains a regular presence in South Dakota, attending community events, meeting with local leaders, and ensuring that the needs of his constituents are always at the forefront of his work in Washington. Looking ahead, Thune's impact on American politics will continue to be felt for years to come. As Senate Majority Leader, he will be in a position to influence the direction of national policy on a wide range of issues, from economic reform to national security and healthcare.

His leadership in the Senate will be crucial in navigating the challenges of a divided Congress and in advancing the Republican agenda in a highly polarized political environment. Thune's legacy, however, will not be defined solely by his policy achievements. It will also be shaped by the way he has conducted himself in office—with dignity, respect for others, and a commitment to upholding the principles of democracy. His reputation as a thoughtful, pragmatic leader who prioritizes the needs of the American people over partisan politics will ensure that his impact extends far beyond his time in office.

John Thune's impact on American politics and the state of South Dakota is both profound and enduring. Through his leadership, advocacy, and commitment to public service, he has shaped the nation's policies on key issues while remaining deeply connected to the needs of his constituents. As he continues to lead the Senate in the years ahead, Thune's influence will continue to shape the political landscape, ensuring that his legacy is one of lasting positive change.

Conclusion

John Thune's career in public service stands as a testament to the enduring power of leadership rooted in integrity, dedication, and a commitment to serving the needs of both his state and his nation. Throughout his tenure in the U.S. House and Senate, Thune has consistently sought to enact policies that advance the well-being of his constituents and the broader American public.

His rise through the ranks of the Senate, culminating in his election as Senate Majority Leader in 2025, marks a significant achievement in a career defined by steady, pragmatic leadership and a deep understanding of the political landscape. As a leader in the Senate, Thune has championed causes that align with his conservative values, particularly on issues of economic policy, energy independence, and national security. His contributions to major legislative achievements such as the Tax Cuts and Jobs Act, as well as his work on infrastructure and technology policy, have cemented his reputation as a powerful force in shaping national policy.

Thune's ability to build bipartisan coalitions and his focus on economic growth and job creation have made him an invaluable asset to his party and a respected figure in Washington, D.C. Thune's commitment to his home state of South Dakota is perhaps one of the most defining aspects of his career. Through his work in both the House and Senate, he has ensured that South Dakota's agricultural industry, rural communities, and veterans receive the support and attention they deserve.

His advocacy for issues such as broadband expansion, infrastructure development, and veteran's benefits have left an indelible mark on the state, providing tangible benefits for generations to come. But beyond his legislative accomplishments, it is Thune's personal values and integrity that truly set him apart. His devotion to family, faith, and service has been a guiding force throughout his career, and these qualities have helped him navigate the challenges of public office while remaining grounded and focused on what matters most. Thune's ability to balance the demands of political life with the need for a strong family foundation has allowed him to maintain a sense of humility and perspective that is often rare in today's hyper-partisan political climate.

As Senate Majority Leader, Thune will undoubtedly face new challenges as he works to guide the Senate through a period of intense political division and national uncertainty. However, his legacy as a leader who strives to put the needs of the American people above partisan politics will continue to guide his actions. Thune's ability to balance principled leadership with the pragmatism required to get things done will be critical as he works to steer the Senate through the complexities of governing in the 21st century.

Looking forward, Thune's influence will continue to be felt in the years to come, both in South Dakota and across the United States. His leadership on key issues such as tax reform, energy policy, and technology will shape the direction of American politics for the foreseeable future. His legacy will be defined not only by the policies he has championed but also by the way he has conducted himself in office—an example of integrity, service, and dedication to the public good. John Thune's career has been a model of effective, principled leadership. His impact on South Dakota and the nation is undeniable, and his continued service in the Senate promises to further strengthen his legacy as one of the most respected figures in American politics.

As he continues to lead the Senate in the coming years, Thune's focus will undoubtedly remain on advancing policies that promote economic growth, protect national security, and improve the lives of all Americans. Through his unwavering dedication to his principles and his constituents, John Thune has proven himself to be a true servant of the people and a leader for the future.

www.ingramcontent.com/pod-product-compliance
Lightning Source LLC
Chambersburg PA
CBHW051838250726

48659CB00005B/1901